WITHOUT
LOVE

A Collection of Songs and Thoughts

Reverend Eric Perry

WESTBOW
PRESS®
A DIVISION OF THOMAS NELSON
& ZONDERVAN

Scripture quotations marked (NIV) are taken from the Holy Bible, New International Version®, NIV®. Copyright © 1973, 1978, 1984, 2011 by Biblica, Inc.™ Used by permission of Zondervan. All rights reserved worldwide. www.zondervan.com The "NIV" and "New International Version" are trademarks registered in the United States Patent and Trademark Office by Biblica, Inc.™

WestBow Press books may be ordered through booksellers or by contacting:

WestBow Press
A Division of Thomas Nelson & Zondervan
1663 Liberty Drive
Bloomington, IN 47403
www.westbowpress.com
1 (866) 928-1240

Because of the dynamic nature of the Internet, any web addresses or links contained in this book may have changed since publication and may no longer be valid. The views expressed in this work are solely those of the author and do not necessarily reflect the views of the publisher, and the publisher hereby disclaims any responsibility for them.

Any people depicted in stock imagery provided by Thinkstock are models, and such images are being used for illustrative purposes only. Certain stock imagery © Thinkstock.

ISBN: 978-1-5127-6286-0 (sc)
ISBN: 978-1-5127-6287-7 (hc)
ISBN: 978-1-5127-6285-3 (e)

Library of Congress Control Number: 2016918488

Print information available on the last page.

WestBow Press rev. date: 11/22/2016

In loving memory of Dana Maria Perry and

Michael L. Gillen

Foreword

Raw is a short word with a deep meaning and multiple nuances. Raw human emotion is intense, unconcealed, unrestrained, passionate, and powerful. Very few people are willing to risk being vulnerable or transparent to the degree their soul is laid open for any and all to see. In this sense, Eric Perry is a raw author, poet, songwriter, and preacher.

In *Without Love*, Pastor Eric invites us to enter into a lifetime of stories filled with joy, sorrow, humor, tragedy, grace, friendship, loss, faith, hope, and love. These stories are woven intricately and carefully with the use of lyrics from a plethora of musical genres, quotes from the sages of time, verses from the Bible, and, of course, Eric's own personal experiences.

In this unique devotional, I found my heart challenged by Eric's many stirring examples of how he humbly fulfilled Jesus's command to "love one another." As Eric shares from his vast vault of adventures, his ability to faithfully love others is so clearly evident. This ability to love both the lovely and the unlovable is an attribute I desire to possess more consistently. It is an attribute our world desperately needs more of.

For the past twenty years, I have walked alongside Eric as a close friend and co-laborer for Christ in ministry. We have hiked together through some of the highest peaks of joy, laughter, and triumphs. We also have meandered across some of the deepest valleys a human heart can enter.

In the midst of it all, I thank God for the backstage pass to witness such a consistent and genuine faith as I have seen in my friend. Even when the circumstances of his life, which he could see, did not make sense, he still trusted in God, whom he could not see.

The love of music is another common bond we share. We talk about groups or performers we enjoy, songs that move us, and memories of concerts we still savor. Music is one of God's greatest gifts, and the use of lyrics in this book is utilized in such an appropriate and timely manner that they always just seem to fit.

"Dr. Perry," as I jokingly call him, has the rare combination of being a thinker and having empathy. He possesses intelligence and common sense. He is a wise man and a wisenheimer.

Eric loves Jesus passionately and has compassion for all people from Detroit to Dessalines, starting with those closest to him, his wife and children. Eric's heart is exposed in his writing and composing like a figurative open-heart surgery. You don't have to be a cardiologist to investigate, but I hope you will because your heart will be stirred as you see a soul moved by the things that move God's heart and will move our hearts.

Reverend Daryl D. Dexter, M. Div.
Pastor, Sherwood Free Methodist Church

Acknowledgments

Dr. Charles White, one of my professors from Spring Arbor University, used to say, "God writes straight with crooked lines." The longer I live, the more I appreciate this statement. My life of following after Jesus has been anything but a straight line with a slight ascent to heaven. It has been filled with potholes, detours, and washouts with some smooth rides in between the rough spots, in a zigzagging sort of way. Maybe you feel the same way about your life.

Like old Bilbo used to say, "It's a dangerous business, Frodo, going out your door. You step into the Road, and if you don't keep your feet, there is no knowing where you might be swept off to." The times I have not been able to keep my feet very well, I have found myself being swept into the loving grace of Jesus. Thank You, Savior.

The thoughts and songs I have shared in this book would not be possible without the amazing people that

God has allowed to cross my path of life in the good and bad times. Some have already received the goal of their faith and are singing in the presence of things too wonderful to imagine.

I am a member of the Southern Michigan Conference of the Free Methodist Church U.S.A., where the fellowship of the cross has been so real. I have received so much from the lives of these Christ followers. The church I pastor, Cornerstone Community Church in Battle Creek, is filled with the precious saints of God, too numerous to mention all, but all are in my heart. Special thanks to Mike Keith, Bill Vale, and Frank Haywood for help when I get stuck on an arrangement, Keith Sherban for his wisdom and Thomas E. Guinn for the use of the Brush Arbor drawing.

I thank God for my wife, Kari, and our combined family: Derick, Anna, Hannah, Christian, Isaac, Jakob and Ellie, Lydia, Jon, Levi, and Cy.

Without Love: Liner Notes

I was born in Battle Creek, Michigan, in 1962. As a young kid growing up, I enjoyed listening to music on the record player and the radio at night. My mom Jan had a wonderful collection of forty-fives. I would play three records over and over again: "Hound Dog" by Elvis Presley, "Long Tall Sally" by Little Richard, and "Hey Good Lookin'" by Hank Williams. These songs were my entry door into the world of music.

On some weekends I would be carted off to my grandmother's house to spend the night, which was always fun. My Grandma Rook was what I call a "Northern hillbilly." She was born in Livingston, Tennessee, but her mother (my great-grandmother) moved to Michigan after her husband (my great-grandfather) was killed. My grandparents would watch the Green Valley Jamboree on Saturday night with Rem Wall and the Green Valley Boys. Rem worked at Gibson Guitar in Kalamazoo and hosted the local TV show. I saw many episodes of the Green Valley Jamboree. They played what I called "hillbilly music."

My grandmother bought me a snare drum when I was eight years old and paid for my lessons from Bill Dowdy, a Battle Creek jazz musician who was well known as a jazz and blues drummer. He used to play for Memphis Slim and Howling Wolf.[1] Battle Creek has had a few musical legends like Junior Walker and the All Stars, Sonny Holley, Willie Woods, and Bill "Stix" Nicks.

Junior Walker and the All Stars were famous for the hit song "Shotgun." Bobby Holley recorded with Stax Records and had a national hit song, "Moving Dancer." Del Shannon hit the charts with "Runaway." Ray Overholt had a gospel hit, "Ten Thousand Angels,"

---

[1] Sonya Bernard-Hollins, *Here I Stand: A Musical History of African Americans in Battle Creek, Michigan* (Kalamazoo, Mich.: Fortitude Graphic Design & Printing, 2003), 120.

that Loretta Lynn also recorded. Frankie Ballard is a young country star. These are just a few of the great musicians from Battle Creek.

My other grandmother, Betty Perry, taught me how to play the organ. I used to go with her to the Congregational church, and the sound of all the pipes from the organ amazed me.

I grew up on Beckley Road. My neighbors were older than I was. Gary Pulsipher, the neighbor on the east, was in high school at the time. I would often hear the Rolling Stones being played from his house. My neighbor on the west, a guy named Brian Blowers, played the coolest set of drums. I took lessons from him as well. He would be playing his drums at night, and I would respond by beating my snare drum.

I-94, the highway that runs from Detroit to Chicago, ran through our backyard. In the summertime, I could hear the garage band at Jimmy Paccuto's house practicing across the highway.

My mom used to book rock bands to come and play at the Lakeview High School summer dances. I could remember seeing Possum Creek, Hot Lucy, Shotgun, and Salem Witchcraft all playing live. It was always fun to go and hear these bands play.

By the time high school rolled around, I had stopped practicing any instrument. I was more interested in hunting my coonhounds and playing football. My friends and I would go to see some of the best rock bands over at the Kalamazoo Wings Stadium, or we would head over to Pine Knob. I saw some great shows there with my brother Rick and my sister Lori. We had a pretty nice sound system, and I would buy albums at places like Shire Records, Choker Records, and later at Crazy Larry's or the Rock Café in Battle Creek. There were cool places too, like Flip Side and Boogie Records in Kalamazoo.

And every time I bought a new album, I couldn't wait to read the liner notes to find out about the songs and who played on the records. Sometimes liner notes offered insight into the lives of my favorite musicians.

While in college I started to play guitar and write my own songs. I took some lessons from local teachers, Ray Brown and Paul Freeburn. After a while, I just would play with people from church. We had a band called the Blood Brothers Blues Band. I played guitar and sang, Mike Henderson was on bass, and Kristen Glubke (a girl) was on drums. We played an outdoor event that got people clapping along. My pastor, Bob Zuhl, took some heat for letting us play rock and roll at a church event. (One of our songs was set to the music of J. J. Cale's song "Cocaine," as Eric Clapton had recorded.) My friend Tim Egan and I would play together at college/singles groups. He is one of the most amazing guitar players I have ever known. He plays a lot like Leo Kottke.

While at Spring Arbor College, I lived in the dorm called O-1 (first floor of Ormston Hall). Good music and musicians always filled this dorm. Mark Glubke had a great classic rock record collection. David Leinweber, a history major from Detroit, could play any song on his guitar. He would play a lot of Eric Clapton and the Allman Brothers. We could name a song, and David could play it. Mike "Psycho" Schneider from Iowa played metal music on a beautiful Dean guitar that he still has today. My roommate Mike Gillen and I had every one of Mylon Lefevre's and Randy Matthews's albums. We had a great dorm.

Every spring, Ormston Hall hosted Porch Fest, which was live music and fun. Mark put together a band for the event. We were called the Flaming Liberals. Mark Glubke was on bass, Dave Leinweber was on guitar, Trevor Mast was on drums, and I sang.

Steve Wilson from Detroit announced us with the opening cadence, "O-1 proudly presents the rockingest blues band from this side of glory, the Flaming Liberals!"

Dave played a mean opening to the Jimi Hendrix song "Red House" on my Gibson Flying V, and that got the crowd rocking. This was a lot of fun. I have a tape of this somewhere.

Most of the songs I write are stories of my life. I grew up with my brother Rick, chasing our bluetick coonhounds through the cornfields, swamps, and woods in Michigan. You could hear the trains at night from the Grand Trunk train yard, miles away in Battle Creek. My father Richard used to work for the Grand Trunk, and he had some good stories about working in the train yard. I love train songs.

I have always loved the swamp music of John Fogerty and Creedence Clearwater Revival and the funky southern boogie and New Orleans sound from Dr. John, Little Feat, the Doobie Brothers, ZZ Top, the Allman Brothers, and Lynyrd Skynyrd. When I heard Skynyrd's "Swamp Music," I would just smile because I lived that song every night. Songs of Jesus, trains, hard times, and life are themes that resonate in my soul.

I decided to put together this little book to share some of my songs and a few thoughts on my life experiences. The phrase "without love" comes from Tom Johnston's song, "Long Train Runnin'," performed by the Doobie Brothers. The following lyric always moves me:

You know I saw Miss Lucy

Down along the track.

She lost her home and her family,

And she won't be coming back.

Without love, where would you be now?[2]

Like you, I have had a few personal "Miss Lucy" experiences, that is, I was broken from life's unexpected

---

[2] Tom Johnston, "Long Train Runnin'," in *The Captain and Me*, Warner/Chappell Music Inc., 1973.

turns. I have found that, over the years, if it were not for the love of God and His people, I would not have made it.

Music has played a large part in the healing of my soul as well. I write this as someone who understands what life along the tracks can be like by someone who has struggled and asked "Why?" when life didn't make sense. But I also know the power of Christ's love shared. And for that, I am thankful. I hope you receive some small encouragement from reading this. Without love, I don't know where I would be today.

As John 3:16 (NIV) says, "For God so loved the world that He gave his one and only Son, that whoever believes in him shall not perish but have everlasting life." How are you doing with your relationship with Jesus?

Bad Times

Jesus said, "In this world you will have trouble.

But take heart! I have overcome the world."

John 16:33 (NIV)

I see a bad moon a-rising. I see trouble on the way.

I see earth quakes and lightnin'.

I see bad times today.[3]

The natural world is full of beauty, hope, and love, as well as hate, pain, violence, and death. The storms of life come, often unannounced and unapologetic. All is not well in our world. No new news here, right? This should not surprise us. After Hurricane Katrina rocked the Louisiana coast in 2005, many homeless people from New Orleans were sent to Fort Custer

---

[3] J. C. Fogerty, "Bad Moon Rising," in *Green River*, Jondora Music BMI, 1969.

Army National Guard Base in Battle Creek/Augusta. Some folks from our church and I went to spend some time there, just talking to people. The stories they shared were terrible. I'll never forget these precious people who saw the water sweeping away loved ones. I prayed with many of these dear souls so God could help them through this disaster.

Psalm 46:1 says, "God is our refuge and strength, an ever present help in trouble." These people needed God's help right away. Unfortunately there will be more storms (trials) in life, but take heart! Jesus never promised us a life free from pain, but He did say He would be with us forever. We all have chances to share the love of Christ with the people around us.

John Fogerty's song "Bad Moon Rising" seems like a prophetic voice, warning of bad times on the way. So you'd better get your things together! Start by trusting in Jesus as your Lord.

Motherless Children

Religion that God our Father accepts as pure and faultless is this: to look after orphans and widows in their distress and to keep oneself from being polluted by the world. James 1:27 NIV

Orphan children has a hard time in this world, Lord
Orphan children has a hard time in this world, Lord
No one cares, they just walk on by+
No one hears the young ravens cry+
Orphan children has a hard time, in this world Lord

Reverend William Johnson, a gospel and blues singer known as Blind Willie Johnson, was born in 1897 in Brenham, Texas. His mother died when he was young, and he wrote the song "Motherless Children." There are different lyrical versions. Many artists have recorded this song, including A. P. Carter, Eric Clapton, and Bob Dylan, to name a few.

Over the years I have traveled to Haiti with my friend, Marv DeVisser, as we took care of the goat herd we helped sponsor through the Friends of Haiti Organization. I love Haiti. The wonderful food, music, and spirit of the Haitian people is awesome. Sometimes I've been there after hurricanes have pounded the country, once after the earthquake in 2010, and again in 2012 with my wife Kari.

My friends, Don and Doris Peavey, run the Ebenezer Glen Orphanage in Dessalines, Haiti. (Don's sister, Frances Roe, is a member of our church. We call her St. Frances.) I traveled to Dessalines to visit the orphanage in 1998 and 2012.

I'll never forget the man who brought a newborn baby, just hours old, to the orphanage. His wife had died from complications of the childbirth. The father had six other children to raise. He sat there, holding this new life while grieving the loss of his wife. My heart broke for this man. Thank God for people like the Peaveys, who care for the orphans in the world.

In 2003, my life was going pretty well. Our church was thriving, our four children were healthy, and we just started the process of adopting a child from Russia. Then something unexpected happened. My wife Dana was diagnosed with breast cancer. After a fourteen-month battle, she went to be with Jesus.

Life changes that fast. There were a lot of days of sadness and struggle afterward. How was I going to raise four children by myself? Children need their parents in their lives, mothers and fathers. Thankfully, the family of God was awesome in helping my children and I adjust to a new life without my wife and their mother.

God hears the cries of the helpless, and He commands His people to look after and care for orphans and widows. Do you know any child who has lost a parent or someone who is widowed? Spend some time encouraging him or her and showing him or her Christ's love.

Jesus said the most important thing we can do is to "Love the Lord your God with all your heart and with all your soul and with all your mind. This is the first and greatest commandment. And the second is like it: Love your neighbor as yourself" Matt. 22:37–39 NIV

Senye (Lord),

Soufrans se wou Pote a (Suffering

is the potter's wheel)

K'ap vire nou nan men Pote a (which

turns us in the Potter's hands)

Ak Kares lanmou (of love and affection).[4]

---

[4] Haitian prayer Elizabeth J Turnbull, God Is No Stranger (Light Messages Durham, North Carolina, 2004) pg. 84

I know of a great ministry that helps children in need around the world. It is the International Childcare Ministries, directed by Dr. Linda Adams. I have seen the awesome work they do in Haiti. Check it out!

Soul Cry

Read Luke 22:39–46

During the days of Jesus' life on earth, he offered up prayers and petitions with loud cries and tears to the one who could save him from death, and he was heard because of his reverent submission." Hebrews 5:7 (NIV)

We cover our deep ignorance with words, but we are ashamed to wonder, we are afraid to whisper 'mystery'.[5]

Sometimes things happen in life that will leave you speechless, events that break our hearts and leave us numb. I remember feeling that way when Dana was diagnosed with breast cancer. Our lives and plans had

---

[5] A. W. Tozer, *The Knowledge of the Holy* (New York: Harper and Row, 1961), 26.

to change. Everyone had an opinion on why this was happening and what we needed to do. We were doing everything we could to please our heavenly Father— serving him, raising our family, and supporting ministries that cared for orphans. Some people think that Christians will never experience hard times. I've never believed followers of Christ are exempt from suffering in this world, as suffering is part of our faith. Dana just looked to Jesus and never took her eyes off Him.

Some folks feel the need to explain everything. I don't. There are things that do not and cannot make sense in our world. Suffering is one of them. It is a mystery. Yes, I know we live in a fallen world. Sin abounds. And God's grace and love are greater. This is true. There have been times in my life that I have needed to pray and there have been no words to pray.

Jesus wrestled in prayer. In the garden of Gethsemane, before he was arrested and crucified, is one example. When Jesus prayed, the Father heard him. He hears your prayers too. If you find it hard at times to pray, don't fret. God prays for us and with us!

"In the same way, the Spirit helps us in our weakness. We do not know what we ought to pray for, but the Spirit himself intercedes for us with groans that words cannot express" (Rom. 8:26 NIV).

Bishop N. T. Wright said, "The message of Gethsemane is loud and clear: do not imagine that because you find yourself in turmoil, struggling with turbulent fear and uncertainty, this means you have come the wrong way or arrived at the wrong place."[6]

"The groans of the dying rise up from the city, and the souls of the wounded cry out for help" (Job 24:12 NIV).

---

[6] N. T. Wright, *The Way of the Lord* (Grand Rapids, Mich.: Eerdmans Publishing, 1999), 89.

Soul Cry (1985)

Reverend Eric Perry

My soul is like a wolf, howling at the moon.

Hear my soul cry, Jesus. Touch my heart real soon.

Oh-oh-oh yeah. Oh, yeah.

My soul is like a wolf, Lord, howling at the moon.

Like the brothers of this tribe, we face trials and pain every day.

Sometimes on my knees at night, I don't know what to pray.

Oh-oh-oh yeah. Oh, yeah.

My soul is like a wolf, Lord, howling at the moon.

The Spirit groans within my soul, which words cannot express.

Not until my soul cries, Jesus, will this warrior get his rest.

Oh-oh-oh yeah. Oh, yeah.

My soul is like a wolf, Lord, howling at the moon.

hear my soul cry Jesus-touch my heart real soon

Pray, children. Pray. And when you don't have the words, do not worry. The Spirit will pray for you with groans that words cannot express.

Port-au-Prince, Haiti

My soul was crushed when I heard the news of the earthquake that shook Haiti on January 12, 2010. Over three hundred thousand people died, including some of the dear people I have met over the years. Dolly DuFour-Peterson, a member of our church, lost her husband Gene, just hours after he arrived in Haiti to do mission work with his friend, Merle West. My friend, Reverend Jeanne Munos, died along with our Haitian brother, Alan Blot. A school just down the road in Delmas 28 collapsed, and over five hundred children died. A church I had preached at in 2008 was completely destroyed. The suffering was so tragic.

I was able to travel back to Haiti later in the year, and I was not sure what to expect. There were a lot of great humanitarian efforts to help the people of Haiti. Actor Sean Penn did an amazing job in helping save people's lives. In the midst of terrible suffering, there was hope. God was there.

My friend, Reverend Marc Andre Pierre, survived with his family. I was so pleased to see his smiling face again. I sat up on the roof of the Bible college and wrote down this song from what I saw and heard taking place on the streets and in the neighborhood of Port-au-Prince, Delmas 28. It is a song of hope.

Senye (Lord),

Si n'ap viv jodi a malgre siklon, grangou, ak malady, nou dwe di

(If we are alive today in spite of hurricanes, hunger and sickness, we should say),

"Mesi, Senye. Nou genle la pou yon bi"

("Thank you, Lord, We must be here for a purpose").[7]

---

[7] Haitian prayer Elizabeth J. Turnbull, God Is No Stranger (Light Messages Durham, North Carolina, 2004), 94.

Port-au-Prince

(Ten Months after the Earthquake)

Reverend Eric Perry

From my rooftop above Port-au-Prince Delmas 28,

I see beautiful things, wonderful things,

Wonderful, beautiful things.

From my rooftop, I see life.

From my rooftop above Port-au-Prince Delmas 28,

I hear beautiful things, wonderful things,

Wonderful, beautiful things.

From my rooftop, I hear life.

From my rooftop above Port-au-Prince Delmas 28,

I see children playing, people working, birds flying,

cars driving.

I hear children laughing, people singing, dogs barking,

Horns honking.

From my rooftop above Port-au-Prince,

From my rooftop above Port-au-Prince,

I praise God.

Why am I a Christian? One reason is the cross of Christ. Indeed, I could never myself believe in God if it were not for the cross. It is the cross that gives God his credibility. In the real world of pain, how could one worship a God who was immune to it?[8]

---

[8] John Stott, *Why I Am a Christian* (Downers Grove, Ill.: Inter Varsity Press, 2003), 62.

Snakebite

Then Jesus was led by the Spirit into the
desert to be tempted by the devil.

Matthew 4:1 (NIV)

So permeated is our nature with the poison of Original Sin that it seeks its own in everything. Not that God made our nature like this, it has become corrupted and disfigured by turning away from him. Johannes Tauler (1300–1361), a German mystic[9]

I remember sitting in my office at church, playing guitar with my friend, David Brummett. Dave, a bass player, at the time worked for Dean Markley in Vicksburg, Michigan, making guitar strings. Dave played in a group called Blue Heaven Gospel Blues Band.

---

[9] Johannes Tauler, *Sermons: The Classics of Western Spirituality* (Mahwah, N.J.: Paulist Press, 1985), 82.

Dave was helping me with a new song I had written, "Snakebite." Dave started laughing when I sang the line, "A devil with a blue dress on is tempting me." The song is about the struggle with temptation and sin. Those words just came out as I played the song for the first time. Dave and his band recorded my song on one of their CDs. It was pretty cool to have someone else singing my song.

"Devil with a Blue Dress" was a hit record for Mitch Ryder and the Detroit Wheels. They were an influence on the great Detroit rockers like Bob Seger and Ted Nugent. I saw Mitch Ryder and the Detroit Wheels in concert. He is such a great singer.

Everyone deals with some type of temptation. Jesus was tempted, yet He did not sin. Being tempted is not the same as sinning. God will provide a way out. Run to Him.

The great German reformer Martin Luther once wrote, "You can't stop the birds from flying over your head. But only let them fly. Don't let them nest in your hair."[10]

"No temptation has seized you except what is common to man. And God is faithful, he will not let you be tempted beyond what you can bear. But when you are tempted he will provide a way out so that you can stand up under it" (1 Cor. 10:13 NIV).

Keep your eyes on Jesus … and your wife. Don't be looking at the devil in a blue dress!

Snakebite (1999)
Reverend Eric Perry

So I say live by the Spirit, and you will not
gratify the desires of the sinful nature. For the
sinful nature desires what is contrary to the
Spirit, and the Spirit what is contrary to the

---

[10] Martin Luther, *By Faith Alone* (Grand Rapids, MI. Word Publishing, Inc., 1998), 67.

sinful nature. They are in conflict with each

other, so that you do not do what you want.

Galatians 5:16–17 (NIV)

Got a snakebite.

Poison's running through my veins.

Got a snakebite.

Poison's running through my veins.

I need a doctor. Lord, I need some medicine

Sinful nature

Is burning inside of me.

Sinful nature

Is burning inside of me.

I need the Savior, Lord, to set me free.

Got a snakebite.

Poison's running through my veins.

Got a snakebite.

Poison's running through my veins.

I need a doctor. Lord, I need some medicine.

Devil with a blue dress on

Is a tempting me.

Devil with a blue dress on

Is a tempting me.

Please, please, please, Jesus, set me free.

"What a wretched man I am! Who will save me from this body of death? Thanks be to God-through Jesus Christ our Lord!" (Rom. 7:24–25 NIV)

Tree'd a Possum

Everyone needs a hobby. I once read that the apostle John raised birds. I like to hunt and write music. I wrote the song, Tree'd a Possum, after seeing Marty Stuart in concert in 2013 at the Blue Gate Theater in Shipshewana, Indiana. It really is a song about my teen years, hanging out with a bunch of coon hunters at the Wolverine State Coon Hunters club in Bellevue, Michigan. Some interesting people would gather at these hunts. Some you could trust; others you couldn't.

Local coonhound legend Dave Dean breeds the northern blue hammer line of coonhounds. I hunted several of Dave's bluetick hounds over the years. It was always fun to go visit him in Dowling, Michigan, and have coffee at his cabin. Dave has a poem in the Hank Williams museum.

Ed Morgan was another great old friend who told some wild tales about growing up in the South. I used to hold church services on Sunday mornings after a coon hunt. It was amazing to see the Spirit of God touching the hearts of these men in unique ways.

I remember when Cas Walker from Tennessee showed up to the club with a truckload of dogs to sell at a night hunt. He had dogs that would run raccoon and possum. Cas owned grocery stores in Tennessee and had a music show. I know Dolly Pardon has credited Cas Walker for letting her play on his show.

In the competition hunts, your dog cannot run anything but a raccoon. Well, if you had a dog that would tree an occasional possum or four, you would be disqualified. Bummer!

One of my best dogs was the world's greatest possum hound! I just got a new bluetick named Northern Blue Zydeco. His swamp music is the music I love.

Tree'd a Possum *(2013)*

Reverend Eric Perry

I took ol' Blue to a coon hunt Saturday night.

I turned him loose; he took off out of sight.

Struck a track, I got to the tree.

There was a grinner smilin' down on me.

Ol' Blue tree'd a possum Saturday night.

Chorus

Hey, Cas Walker, you got the best of me.

Said Blue was the brag dog of the state of Tennessee.

There's frost on the pumpkin.

My ego took a thump'n. Ol' Blue tree'd a possum
Saturday night.

I'd whip old Blue, but I guess he's a lot like me.

He and I ain't always what we ought to be.

If he'd tree a coon just one day,

I'd be in church on Sunday.

And then I know Jesus smiled down on me.

Chorus

Hey, Cas Walker, you got the best of me.

Said Blue was the brag dog of the state of Tennessee.

There's frost on the pumpkin.

My ego took a thump'n. Ol' Blue tree'd a possum

Saturday night.

North Star Freedom

"So if the Son sets you free, you will
be free indeed" (John 8:36 NIV).

Sojourner Truth

One of my proudest moments came in 1997 when
I was asked to play my song "North Star Freedom"
during the two-hundredth anniversary celebration of
the birth of Sojourner Truth, whose birth name was
Isabella Baumfree. Sojourner was a black abolitionist
and women's rights activist who was born into slavery

in Ulster County, New York. She escaped slavery in 1826 with her infant daughter.

Sojourner spoke boldly on many issues. Amazingly this woman had met with President Lincoln and once challenged a discouraged Frederick Douglass with this statement, "Frederick, is God dead?" Sojourner Truth lived and died in Battle Creek. She is buried in Oak Hill Cemetary, and there is a wonderful statue of her as you enter Battle Creek on the corner of M-66 and Michigan Avenue.

Another great woman abolitionist was Harriet Tubman, or Sister Moses, the famous conductor on the Underground Railroad. She followed the North Star and led many slaves to freedom. I honor the courage of these two black American women.

I played my song "North Star Freedom" at the Chautauqua event during her celebration. The Chautauqua was an adult education movement in the United States that was highly popular in the late nineteenth and early twentieth centuries. Chautauqua assemblies expanded and spread throughout rural America until the mid-1920s. The Chautauqua brought entertainment and culture for the whole community with speakers, teachers, musicians, entertainers, and preachers.

Modern-day slavery still exists in our world. An estimated 46 million people are enslaved globally. We need brave people like Harriet Tubman and Sojouner Truth to fight against this evil.

North Star Freedom (1997)

Reverend Eric Perry

In honor of Sojourner Truth and Harriet Tubman

Headed up north on a midnight train,
they rode the Underground Railroad
all the way to Michigan.
Men, women, and children with nothing left to lose

ran from the chains (South).

They were sojourners of truth.

Done pick'n cotton,

I'll feel the master's whip no more.

Done pick'n cotton,

I'll feel the master's whip no more,

riding North Star freedom all the way to heaven's door.

North Star freedom, shine your light on me.

North Star freedom, shine your light on me.

Trust now in Jesus. He can set you free.

Tonight we'll follow Sister Moses north to the Promised

Land.

We'll follow Sister Moses north to the Promised Land.

Cry out to Jesus. Lord, take me by the hand.

Isabella went, and she talked to the president.

Isabella went, and she talked to the president.

Please, Mr. Lincoln, help us if you can.

Check out the Set Free Movement. This is a modern day abolitionist group led by Kevin Austin.

Fried Chicken Evangelism

While Jesus was having dinner at Matthew's house, many tax collectors and 'sinners' came and ate with him and his disciples. When the Pharisees saw this, they asked his disciples, 'Why does your teacher eat with tax collectors and sinners?'" (Matt. 9:10–11 NIV).

My maternal great-grandmother was a devout follower of Jesus. She was from Livingston, Tennessee. Her maiden name was Evelyn Stout, and she married Horace Poston, who was tragically killed and left her with two young girls to raise, my grandmother Hortense Leah and her sister Zenoba Dixie.

My great-grandmother moved up north to Michigan to get a job to support her family. She remarried Olin Jenney and lived on a farm. She faithfully attended the Fredonia Holiness Church in Ceresco, Michigan.

When it got harder for her to drive, she used to call me up and ask me to take her to church. She said, if I took her to church, she would "knock a tater in the head and fry me a chicken." Her bribe worked. She made the best fried chicken in the world!

Jesus ate with lost people. What better way to share God's grace with people than over a dinner? I think my great-grandmother was just doing her best to share Jesus's love with me. If you make a fried chicken dinner and invite Jesus over, He will always show up. Jesus loves fried chicken and lost people! "Here I am! I stand at the door and knock. If anyone hears my voice and opens the door, I will come in and eat with him, and he with me" (Rev. 3:20 NIV).

A Table Set for Three (2015)

Reverend Eric Perry

In memory of my Grandma Jenney

There was a table set for three in my grandma's kitchen.

She'd knock a tater in the head and fry us up a chicken.

Although the table was set for three,

it was just my grandma and me.

By the end of the meal, we were joined by Jesus.

Born and raised near Stout Mountain, Tennessee,

she was widowed young and moved up North to raise

her family.

My grandma was not famous; my grandma was not

well known.

My grandma loved Jesus; my grandma loved God's

Word.

There was a table set for three in my grandma's kitchen.

She'd knock a tater in the head and fry us up a chicken.

Although the table was set for three,

it was just my grandma and me.

By the end of the meal, we were joined by Jesus.

My grandma would call me up on a Saturday night,

"Honey, if you take me to church, I'll make it right."

When the service was over at the Fredonia Holiness church,

I took my grandma back home, and she made me my lunch.

There was a table set for three in my grandma's kitchen.

She'd knock a tater in the head and fry us up a chicken.

Although the table was set for three,

it was just my grandma and me.

By the end of the meal, we were joined by Jesus.

The Bluesman

I've always enjoyed listening to blues music. It was the first style I wanted to learn when I started playing guitar. I had a group called the Blood Brothers Blues Band. I also played using the name Junker George. I have seen some great blues players like Buddy Guy, Albert Collins, Johnny Winter, Billy Gibbons, Eric Clapton, and Robert Cray, to name a few.

During my first year at Spring Arbor College, we got to spend the weekend at the Olive Branch Mission in Chicago, the oldest mission in that city. Free Methodist ladies established the mission in the 1800s. We had a free night to do what we wanted, so I checked the *Chicago Tribune* for music events. Junior Wells was playing at the Checkerboard Lounge. I had to go!

No one wanted to go with me, so I got a ride. I was the only white boy in the place. I felt at home when

Junior came over to my table and shook my hand. That was a blast. Buddy Guy came out and played James Brown's "Living in America" at the end of Junior's set. I saw Buddy Guy again at an outdoor concert in Battle Creek a few years later. He is a great bluesman.

My love for music has allowed me to meet people all over. In 1982 and 1983, my friend Chris Jakway and I spent several weeks in Jamaica. We did a couple programs with a Jamaican group called the Gospel Satellites. One of the singer's names was Elvis Presley. It's true! Chris and I used to walk over to the Tuff Gong Studio and talk with people who knew Bob Marley. This was about a year and a half after Bob had died.

I was recently listening to a Stevie Ray Vaugh song, "Tin Pan Alley." Honestly, it made me cry. It is just so gut-wrenching, filled with heartache and hopelessness, the raw human condition. Only the Savior of the world, Jesus Christ, can heal this type of brokenness. He is the only hope. He is the real bluesman who understands the sin-sick souls of fallen humanity. He gave his life on the cross to save and heal lost humankind. I hope you have trusted in Jesus.

"God made you alive with Christ. He forgave us all our sins … he took it away, nailing it to the cross" (Col. 2:13–14 NIV).

The Bluesman (1985)

Reverend Eric Perry

If anyone would come after me, he must deny himself and take up his cross and follow me.
Mark 8:34 (NIV)

The bluesman he walks
down the road every day.
He has no money,
no place to stay.

He is a man of sorrows,

familiar with pain.

He walks into town

with guitar in his hand.

People gather around

to hear the bluesman.

He plays the blues

like there's nails in his hands.

Smitten and afflicted,

Beaten and bruised,

Crown of thorns on his head,

He went to the cross for you.

You can't run; you can't turn away

with each note that he plays.

Hear the bluesman sing.

Pick up the cross. Come and follow me.

"He was despised and rejected by men, a man of sorrows and familiar with suffering … he was pierced for our transgressions, he was crushed for our iniquities, the punishment that brought us peace was upon him" (Isa. 53 NIV).

Comin' Home

Read Luke 15:11–32

You left your hometown for the city lights,

You were young and you were strong

Lots of traffic lots of sleepless nights,

Lots of dreams that all went wrong

You'll just tell them what they want to

hear, How you took the place by storm

You won't tell them how you lost it all,

You'll just say your comin' home.[11]

Being from Michigan, I grew up listening to Bob Seger, who has written so many classic rock songs. One of my favorites, "Comin' Home," comes from his album, *The Distance*. Check it out. It is a story of

---

[11] Bob Seger, "Comin' Home," in *The Distance*, Gear Publishing Co., 1979, 1983.

someone who chased his or her dreams, only to have them unfulfilled and broken. Like the Prodigal Son, the person decides to go back home. Hopefully, home is a place where you can find love again.

We have all experienced broken dreams or have been hurt in relationships by people we trusted. Maybe the job you thought would always be there dried up and you were no longer needed. I have pastored a church on the edge of town for almost twenty years. At our church, I have seen people who have been bruised by life come and go and then come back again. We offer a place to be loved by God and restored to Jesus. If you find yourself at this place in life, know you are deeply loved by the God who created you. Jesus loves you, and you can always come home to him.

Here is a trustworthy saying that deserves full acceptance, "Christ Jesus came into the world to save sinners-of whom I am the worst" (1 Tim. 1:15 NIV).

Hit the Sawdust Trail

An old brush arbor

Old brush arbors by the side of the road

Where the mighty light of God's great mercy flowed

There was praying shouting singing

Till the country side was ringing

Brush arbors by the side of the road

Old brush arbors by the side of the road[12]

---

[12] Darrell Edwards and Gordon Ardis, "Old Brush Arbors," in
I'm a People, Columbia, 1965. (George Jones recorded the song.)

Bill Wolfe, a dear friend, attended our church for several years before he went home to Jesus. Bill, who was born and raised in Arkansas, shared some great stories about growing up in the countryside and attending revival meetings in Brush Arbors. Like the old tent revival meetings, they used to cover the center aisle with sawdust to keep the dust down as people walked down to the altar to pray and get things right with Jesus. People were said to have "hit the sawdust trail" in repentance. What a great memory to have.

I met Jesus on a Sunday night, August 31, 1980, at the Lakeview High football field. Reverend Clyde Dupin, an evangelist from Kernersville, North Carolina, was holding a citywide crusade. I got a phone call that invited me to the meeting at seven twenty-seven that night. During the week, my longtime childhood friend, Mike Pape, was getting ready to leave for college at the University of Michigan. He showed me in the Bible how to be saved and explained what that meant. All week long I was feeling the need to trust in Jesus.

Dr. Dupin preached about Jesus being God's one and only Son. I did not have a problem believing that God existed. My issue was my sin. I was not on a good path. I was going to end up in hell. Dr. Dupin said Jesus died for my sins and all I needed was to believe in Jesus and know that his death on the cross was for my sins.

He was right. As the preacher closed in prayer and the choir sang "Just as I Am," I got up out of my bleacher seat and went forward to pray. I hit the sawdust trail. The son of an old coon hunting friend, Doug Stanton, was in the choir and saw me come forward. He came down from the choir and prayed with me as I asked Jesus into my heart. It does not matter where you are or what your story is. Jesus loves you. If you want to follow him, pray to Jesus, and ask him to be your Lord.

In the summer of 2015, I saw John Mellencamp and Carlene Carter in concert at the Detroit Opera House. It was a great show. John's *Scarecrow* album is on my top-ten favorite list. John told the story of visiting his grandmother, who was nearly a hundred years old. She calls him Buddy.

He said he went to see her, and she took him by the hand and prayed for them, "Lord, it is time for Buddy and me to come home."

John said he got nervous because he was not following the Lord like she was and he had some more sinning to do. The story was cute from Grandma's side, yet I felt saddened for Mr. Mellencamp. He is a great singer and songwriter. I have enjoyed and respected his music for decades. By his own admission, he was not ready to meet Jesus. Are you?

Each of us will die someday, and then we will see Jesus. What will we say? There is nothing on earth worth forfeiting your soul and salvation for. Nothing.

I am glad I had people who prayed for me and told me about Jesus. Homecoming day will be a great celebration because of Jesus. Jesus is the only way to heaven. We need to trust in Him.

Here I am, almost thirty-six years later, still following after Jesus. I certainly never dreamed of becoming a preacher on that night of August 31! And even though there are unanswered questions in my life, I have seen God do some amazing things. My hope is that you will believe in Jesus Christ. All you need is faith. Just get on board!

"Find a good Bible-believing church to attend, and read the gospel of John." That's the advice I was given on August 31, 1980. Jesus has changed everything! There is no reason for anyone to live "without love."

"But these are written that you may believe that Jesus is the Christ, the Son of God, and that by believing you may have life in his name" (John 20:31 NIV).

The Welkin Ringers "Woo Hoo" Jubilee Band

Read Luke 15:1–7 (NIV)

The LORD your God is with you, He is mighty
to save. He will take great delight in you. He
will quite you with his love, he will rejoice
over you with singing. Zephaniah 3:17 (NIV)

God sings! The translated Hebrew phrase "He will
rejoice over you with singing" can also be translated
literally as "He rejoices over you with a shout of joy." I
know what you're thinking. God could not possibly be
rejoicing over the things I have done. It's true. All of
us have sinned. God looks at you through the eyes of
Christ's work on the cross. He loves you. While some
may sadly reject His gift of grace, you don't have to.
The Lord shouts "woo hoo" in heaven every time a

sinner turns in faith to Jesus. We'd better follow his example!

Welkin is an Old English word for the heavens or sky. Charles Wesley used this originally in his classic Christmas hymn, "Hark! How All the Welkin Rings." His friend George Whitefield changed the wording to "Hark! The Herald Angels Sing." Wesley used the word to describe the angelic celebration in the sky over Bethlehem on the night of the birth of our Savior, Jesus Christ.

I have had the opportunity to be a pastor for over twenty years. During these years I have seen an amazing mixture of musical talent as a part of our worship. They have called themselves the Cornerstone Crew because the name of our church is Cornerstone. I am starting a new band made up of "saints below and saints above" called the Welkin Ringers "Woo Hoo" Jubilee Band! You are invited to join!

A Swedish proverb says, "Those who wish to sing, always find a song."

Iron Horse Rolling Songbook

Junker George and the Lafayette
St. Junkyard Band
Iron Horse Rolling

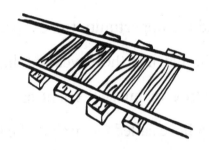

1. Michigan Steel

2. Angelique and the Loup Garou

3. Soul Cry

4. Your Wanted Man

5. Snakebite

6. North Star Freedom

7. Tree'd a Possum

8. Table Set for Three

9. Port-au-Prince

10. Eye of the Gator

11. How Do I Pray for an Angel?

12. Mean Old Train Blues

13. Fond du Lac- Cadillac

Songs inspired by Junker George

Written by Eric Perry

Produced by Pere Detroit

Copyright 2016 Gator Eye Music

Junker George

I once sold a bluetick coonhound puppy to a man named Mr. Toussaint. He drove a big, white Cadillac. His wife, a very sweet lady, said he was going to baby his hound dog. And he did. The dog rode around town in that Cadillac. Mr. Toussaint owned a garage downtown, and I would drive by there from time to time. Blue would be sleeping on one of the old cars in the lot.

I once stopped to talk to Mr. Toussaint and see the dog. Mr. Toussaint was not there, but a man named Junker George was. He said his name was Luther, but everyone called him Junker George. He started telling me about an old redbone hound he and his father owned. They used to hunt coon and possum where he grew up in Louisiana.

Junker George was born and raised in Lafayette, Louisiana. A mechanic, he worked in a garage for his father. He moved up North to Detroit after World War II to work in the Ford steel mill called the Rouge. Junker George only had the use of one arm. He said, when he was a little boy, his grandpa's brother took him gator hunting in the swamp, and an alligator tried to eat him.

Mr. Toussaint told me that Luther injured his arm while working in the steel mill. Luther was actually Mr. Toussaint's brother-in-law, and he lived with Toussaints. His full name was Luther Neville. Luther's grandfather, a country preacher, gave him the nickname Junker George after the German Protestant reformer, Martin Luther. Luther had a blues band called Junker George and the Lafayette St. Junkyard Band. He used to sing and play harmonica. He was great. He sounded like an old freight train.

Luther had some interesting friends. He used to live in the Detroit "Down River" region while he worked at the Rouge steel mill. He talked often of St.

Elmo, who was "Muskrat French." He, along with his father, used to provide muskrat for the Catholic people to eat during Lent. Then there was Pere Detroit and a man he called "Crazy Red," who claimed to have seen the Nain Rouge (red dwarf) along the shore of the Detroit River.

I met Pere Detroit, and we are friends. He is almost a hundred years old. He has a sharp mind, and he loves Jesus and playing the guitar and fiddle. We call our music Northern Blue Zydeco when we get together to play. We wished Clifton Chenier could have joined us!

When I left for college, I stopped down to the garage to say good-bye to Junker George. He smiled and wished me well. That was the last time I saw Luther. He ended up going back to Louisiana to live with his daughter in New Orleans, and he eventually died in 1987.

I learned to play guitar while I was in college. I tried to play the songs like I heard Junker George sing.

He used to say, "Songs are a gift from the Lord, and you need to play them with all your heart." I still hear Junker George playing his harmonica every time a train rolls through town.

Junker George inspired me. I've done my best to honor the memories of my dear friend, Luther Neville. Junker George lives in this music. Special thanks to Pere Detroit for all the encouragement over the years.

Michigan Steel

Eric Perry

A

Iron ore taken from the Marquette range

                                                   E

Iron ore loaded on the freighter boat

A

Big laker sailing through the Soo locks

B   A   E   B7

Big laker all the way to Detroit

Iron ore taken to the steel mills

Iron ore taken to the Rouge

Big three making all your favorite trucks

Big three: GM, Chrysler, and Ford

Iron horse rolling across America

Iron horse pulling loaded freight cars

Freight cars loaded with your favorite trucks

Made in Michigan: Chevy, Dodge, and Ford

Made in Michigan with Michigan steel

Made in Michigan by Michigan steel

Angelique and the Loup Garou

Eric Perry

E   A

I've got a song you about a Loup Garou

E   B7

and a French girl, Angelique.

E   A

She grew up on her papa's farm

E   B7   E

outside of Fort Detroit.

All the local boys would stop and stare

as lovely Angelique walked by.

She had raven hair and skin so fair.

She was the prettiest girl alive.

Chorus

Angelique, beware.

There's a wolf out there

dressed up like a habitant.

A Loup Garou, he's got his eye on you.

He wants to steal you to the swamp.

On the winter nights, pretty Angelique

would sit by the fire and sing.

She'd sing to la bon Dieu.

She cooked la poisson blanc soup.

It stirred up the Loup Garou.

One spring night, young Philippe

fell in love with Angelique.

She danced la gigue a deux

underneath the moon,

being watched by the Loup Garou.

Chorus

The wedding day came,

and the church bells rang.

A wolf strolled through the crowd that day,

an uninvited guest.

The crazy French Loup

came and stole Angelique away.

Soul Cry

Eric Perry

Slow blues in E

My soul is like a wolf, howling at the moon.

Hear my soul cry, Jesus. Touch my heart real soon.

Oh-oh-oh yeah. Oh, yeah.

My soul is like a wolf, Lord, howling at the moon.

Like the brothers of this tribe, we face trials and pain
every day.

Sometimes on my knees at night, I don't know what
to pray.

Oh-oh-oh yeah. Oh, yeah.

My soul is like a wolf, Lord, howling at the moon.

The Spirit groans within my soul, which words cannot
express.

Not until my soul cries, Jesus, will this warrior get his rest.

Oh-oh-oh yeah. Oh, yeah.

My soul is like a wolf, Lord, howling at the moon.

Hear my soul cry, Jesus. Touch my heart real soon.

Your Wanted Man

Eric Perry

Slow ballad

G

I'm not Jesse James.

Em

I've never robbed a train.

C

I'm just doing my best

D

to steal your heart

C   G

and be your wanted man.

I'll do whatever it takes.

I'll stage the perfect jail break.

Reverend Eric Perry

Please take the chains off your heart.
Let me start, being your wanted man.

When you walked through the door,
my heart began to pound
like a buffalo stampede.
You shook me off my feet.
Please let me be your wanted man.

My horse is waiting outside.
Come on, baby. We can ride
into the sunset,
if you just let me be your
wanted man.

Snakebite

Eric Perry

E7   Eaug9

Got a snakebite.

Poison's running through my veins.

    A

Got a snakebite.

             E7

Poison's running through my veins.

B7   A   E7

I need a doctor, Lord. I need some medicine.

Sinful nature

is burning inside of me.

Sinful nature,

is burning inside of me.

I need the Savior, Lord, to set me free.

Got a snakebite.

Poison's running through my veins.

Got a snakebite.

Poison's running through my veins.

I need a doctor, Lord. I need some medicine.

Devil with a blue dress on

is a tempting me.

Devil with a blue dress on

is a temping me.

Please, please, please, Jesus set me free.

North Star Freedom

Eric Perry

E

Headed up north on a midnight train,

they rode the Underground Railroad

all the way to Michigan.

A   E   E7

Men, women, and children with nothing left to lose

B7

ran from the chains (South).

A   E   E7

They were sojourners of truth.

Done pick'n cotton,

I'll feel the master's whip no more.

Done pick'n cotton,

I'll feel the master's whip no more,

riding North Star freedom all the way to heaven's door.

Chorus

North Star freedom, shine your light on me.

North Star freedom, shine your light on me.

Trust now in Jesus. He can set you free.

Tonight we'll follow Sister Moses north to the Promised Land.

We'll follow Sister Moses north to the Promise Land.

Cry out to Jesus, Lord. Take me by the hand.

Isabella went, and she talked to the president.

Isabella went, and she talked to the president.

Please, Mr. Lincoln, help us if you can.

Tree'd a Possum

Eric Perry

A   E   A

I took ol' Blue to a coon hunt Saturday night.

A   E   B7

I turned him loose. He took off out of sight.

D   A

Struck a track, I got to the tree.

D   A

There was a grinner smilin' down on me.

D   A   E   A

Ol' Blue tree'd a possum Saturday night.

Hey, Cas Walker, you got the best of me.

Said Blue was the brag dog of the state of Tennessee.

There's frost on the pumpkin

My ego took a thump'n. Ol' Blue tree'd a possum

Saturday night.

I'd whip old Blue, but I guess he's a lot like me.

He and I ain't always what we ought to be.

If he'd tree a coon just one day,

I'd be in church on Sunday.

And then I know Jesus smiled down on me.

Hey, Cas Walker, you got the best of me.

Said Blue was the brag dog of the state of Tennessee.

There's frost on the pumpkin.

My ego took a thump'n. Ol' Blue tree'd a possum

Saturday night.

Port-au-Prince

Eric Perry

Caribbean feel

D

From my rooftop above Port-au-Prince-Delmas 28,

D   G   D   G   D

I see beautiful things, wonderful things,

G   D   A

wonderful, beautiful things.

A   D

I see life.

From my rooftop above Port-au-Prince-Delmas 28,

I hear beautiful things, wonderful things,

wonderful, beautiful things.

From my rooftop, I hear life.

From my rooftop above Port-au-Prince-Delmas 28,

I see children playing, people working, birds flying, cars driving.
I hear children laughing, people singing, dogs barking, horns honking.

From my rooftop above Port-au-Prince,
From my rooftop above Port-au-Prince,
I praise God.

A Table Set for Three

Eric Perry

C   G

There was a table set for three in my grandma's kitchen.

                                                                   C

She'd knock a tater in the head and fry us up a chicken.

Although the table was set for three,

F

it was just my grandma and me.

G   C

By the end of the meal, we were joined by Jesus.

G   C

Born and raised near Stout Mountain, Tennessee,

G   C

she was widowed young and moved up North to raise

her family.

F

My grandma was not famous. My grandma was not well known.

G   C

My grandma loved Jesus. My grandma loved God's Word.

Chorus

There was a table set for three in my grandma's kitchen.

She'd knock a tater in the head and fry us up a chicken.

Although the table was set for three,

it was just my grandma and me.

By the end of the meal, we were joined by Jesus.

My grandma would call me up on a Saturday night,

"Honey, if you take me to church, I'll make it right."

When the service was over at the Fredonia Holiness church,

I took my grandma back home, and she made me my
lunch.

There was a table set for three in my grandma's kitchen.
She'd knock a tater in the head and fry us up a chicken.
Although the table was set for three,
it was just my grandma and me.
By the end of the meal, we were joined by Jesus.

Eye of the Gator

Eric Perry

E   E7

Bayou living in Louisiana swamp

E   E7

Eye of the gator looking for a bite

E   E7

Crawdaddy playing in his Zydeco band

E   E7

Hungry old gator got his eye on him

A

Moon shining bright on the bayou tonight

E   B7

Eye of the gator looking for a bite (moon so bright)

A   E   E7

Crawdaddy has to wear his shades

Bayou living in Louisiana swamp

Eye of the gator looking for a bite

Bullfrog singing the bullfrog blues

Hungry old gator got his eye on him too

Moon so bright on the bayou tonight

Eye of the gator looking for a bite (moon so bright)

Bullfrog has to wear his shades

Bayou living in Louisiana swamp

Eye of the gator looking for a bite

Pere Detroit fiddling Cajun tunes

Hungry old gator got his eye on him

Moon so bright on the bayou tonight

Eye of the gator looking for a bite (moon so bright)

Pere Detroit has to wear his shades

Bayou living in Louisiana swamp

Eye of the gator looking for a bite

Junker George playing the accordion

Reverend Eric Perry

Hungry old gator got his eye on him

Moon so bright on the bayou tonight

Eye of the gator looking for a bite (moon so bright)

Junker George has to wear his shades

How Do I Pray for an Angel?

Eric Perry

G   C   G

Holding hands as we sit on your front porch

     G   C   D

Making plans for our life and days to come

     G   C   G

Almost a year since we met last December

                    D   G

That's when an angel appeared from above

         C   G

Dear Lord, how do I pray for an angel?

      C   D

Because I know there's one sitting by my side

 G   C Cm

Oh, Jesus, I'm holding hands with an angel—Yes,
I am—

        G   D   G

this beautiful woman, the love of my life.

It was a sacred day at the Silent Night chapel

when I knelt down and asked you to marry me.

You said yes with all heaven's approval.

We felt His presence surround us all day.

Dear Lord, how do I pray for an angel?

Because I know there's one sitting by my side.

Oh, Jesus, I'm holding hands with an angel—Yes,

I am—

this beautiful woman, the love of my life.

So here we stand before God at this altar,

exchanging vows. You'll wear my wedding ring.

With seeking hearts and eyes fixed on Jesus,

my precious angel, it will all be okay.

Mean Old Train Blues

Eric Perry

Upbeat in E

All alone in New Orleans …

Baby is Yazoo City bound.

All alone in New Orleans …

Baby is Yazoo City bound.

Mean old train just left the station,

whistle laughing at me out loud.

Baby said her sister needs her.

Lord, what am I going to do?

Said her sister needs her.

Lord, what am I going to do?

Mean old train just left the station,

singing the mean old train blues.

Got your trail here in New Orleans.

My bloodhound's on your track.

Your steel rails stole my baby.

My bloodhound's on your track.

Mean old train, I'm gonna hunt you

'til I get my baby back.

Illinois Central,

you used to be my friend.

Illinois Central,

you used to be my friend.

Mean old train, you took my woman.

Please bring her home to me again.

Many train songs deal with love taken away by a train. Check out John Lee Hooker's "Mean Old Train" and Cecil Gant's song, "Train Time Blues." Lightnin' Slim sang "Mean Ole Lonesome Train," and B.B. King had "Mean Ole Frisco." My song uses the phrase "mean old train," but it has a different story to it.

Fond du Lac-Cadillac

Eric Perry

Acapella

I never will forget that summer day
at Fond du Lac-Cadillac.
I saw St. Lucy walking down the beach
at Fond du Lac-Cadillac.
Her long, blonde hair was blowing in the wind
at Fond du Lac-Cadillac
with Swedish blue eyes and pale white skin
at Fond du Lac-Cadillac.

I got up the courage to ask her name
at Fond du Lac-Cadillac.
She said she lived across the street
at Fond du Lac-Cadillac.
We walked all day, and I held her hand

at Fond du Lac-Cadillac.

As the sun went down, my heart began to sink

at Fond du Lac-Cadillac.

She said she had to go. It was getting late

at Fond du Lac-Cadillac.

The full moon lit up the starry sky

over Fond du Lac-Cadillac.

Before we left, I kissed her good-bye

at Fond du Lac-Cadillac.

I prayed to the Father that I'd make it back

to Fond du Lac-Cadillac.

I just had to see St. Lucy again

at Fond du Lac-Cadillac,

at Fond du Lac-Cadillac.

"Fond du Lac" is a French term meaning, the "farthest end of the lake."

Printed in the United States
By Bookmasters